Is God Real to You?

Lessons for Teen Girls

OTHER LESSONS FOR TEEN GIRLS
BY JACLYNN WEBER

No Regrets

Do It Right the First Time!

Is God Real to You?

JACLYNN WEBER

Christian Womanhood
8400 Burr Street
Crown Point, Indiana 46307
(219) 365-3202
www.christianwomanhood.org

ISBN: 0-9793892-3-2

All Scriptures used in this book are
from the King James Bible.

CREDITS:
Cover Design: Jaclynn Weber
Page Layout: Linda Stubblefield
Proofreading: Rena Fish, Jane Grafton,
and Cindy Schaap

Printed in the United States of America

Table of Contents

Footprints

ONE NIGHT A MAN had a dream. He dreamed he was walking along the beach with the Lord. Across the sky flashed scenes from his life. For each scene, he noticed two sets of footprints in the sand—one belonging to him and the other to the Lord.

When the last scene of his life flashed before him, he looked back at the footprints in the sand. He noticed that many times along the path of his life there was only one set of footprints. He also noticed that it happened at the very lowest and saddest times in his life.

This really bothered him, and he questioned the Lord about it. "Lord, You said that once I decided to follow You, You'd walk with me all the way. But I have noticed that during the most troublesome times in my life, there is only one set of footprints. I don't understand why when I needed You most, You would leave me."

The Lord replied, "My son, My precious child, I love you, and I would never leave you. During your times of trial and suffering, when you see only one set of footprints, it was then that I carried you."

– Author unknown

CHAPTER ONE

Why?

WHY? A QUESTION WE ask ourselves, others, and God over and over again, but a question for which we never really seem to find any answers.

Why? An almost bitter cry to God at times because we feel that He has been unfair to us or has not treated us like we feel we should have been treated.

Why? The dejected way we try to analyze others who have hurt us or who have rejected our love and emotion, sometimes through tears of anger or of a broken heart.

Why? Our heart's way of handling pain and grief in moments of regret or sadness as we reflect on the way things could have been or maybe should have been in the past.

Why? There are a thousand "whys" that we could

ask, and I have asked many at times in my own life. The only bad thing about asking "Why?" is that no matter how many times you ask it or how angry or sad you are when you ask it, your "Why?" will never be answered.

There have been many moments in my life when I have looked up to Heaven through tears of anger, frustration, or sadness, and I have asked God, "Why did You allow this to happen to me?" There have been other times when I have said to myself, "Why did you ever do that?" There have also been other times when I looked at others and said to myself, "Why did they do that to me? Did they mean to hurt me?"

When my grandpa died, I remember asking the question "Why?" a lot, and I wondered if God really knew what He was doing. During my high school days and during a particularly rough year, I remember going home at night and asking "Why?" I have asked myself why I have been so stupid sometimes and have not used my head before I plunged into something I came to later regret. I am sure Dr. Wendell Evans, the president of Hyles-Anderson College, and my grandmother, Mrs. Beverly Hyles, the wife of the late Dr. Jack Hyles, have asked "Why?" many times in trying to understand why they were each left without a mate. I am sure Mr. Reed Brock, who has a daughter Kimberly who is blind and a son David who is handicapped and whose wife Bonnie recently suffered a stroke, has asked "Why?"

I have asked a thousand "whys" and probably most of you reading this book have, too. If your questions have been like mine, I have never had anyone explain to me why my problems have happened, and I cannot even answer the "whys" I have asked myself.

Well, I guess there is only one thing I can do. If my questions are not going to get answered even though I keep asking them, then I guess I'll have to put my trust in the only One Who does know the answers. You guessed it—I have to put my trust in God.

I like to sing a song that reminds me to trust in God and not ask questions. It makes me realize that Jesus knows everything about me and that He promised to take care of me every day for the rest of my life.

That song goes like this:

I don't know about tomorrow,
I just live from day to day.

I don't borrow from its sunshine,
For its skies may turn to gray.
I don't worry o'er the future,
For I know what Jesus said,
And today He'll walk beside me,
For He knows what is ahead.

Many things about tomorrow
I don't seem to understand,
But I know Who holds tomorrow,
And I know Who holds my hand.

I want you to read these words carefully, and whenever you want to ask "Why?" remind yourself that God is the only One Who knows the answer and decide you are going to trust in Him.

Trust. A decision to believe in Someone or something you cannot see.

Trust. To put your faith in God instead of asking "Why?"

Trust. Giving your heart and soul to Someone Who you know loves you very much and on whom you can count to be there for you—no matter what you go through.

Trust. *"It is better to trust in the* LORD *than to put confidence in man."* (Psalm 118:8)

I choose today to trust God instead of spending my life trying to find out the answers to "Why?" because no matter what comes my way, "I know Who holds tomorrow, and I know Who holds my hand."

CHAPTER TWO

Why Do I Have to Be a Preacher's Daughter?

AS A PREACHER'S DAUGHTER, I was pretty much a typical teenager. I wanted to be popular, wear stylish clothes, have lots of friends, and date lots of guys. However, no matter how hard I tried to be like everyone else, I never felt like I completely "fit in." I knew that I was no better and no worse than anyone else, yet I felt like people expected more out of me than they did the "normal" kids. Preachers' kids, let's face it: people at your church and school do watch you more than normal, and they do expect more out of you than they do from "Joe" who just got saved and came to church for the first time.

When I was in junior high, we had a Bible verse

theme for our school that I remember seeing posted in the classroom of Mrs. Debbie Borsh, one of my teachers, *"For unto whomsoever much is given, of him shall be much required."* (Luke 12:48b) I think of that verse often when I start to feel sorry for myself, that I have this heavy "burden" of being a preacher's (and now a pastor's) daughter. The truth is I have been given a lot more than I deserve and more than many other people have, but that also means that God is going to require a lot out of me.

When I was seven years old, my dad started a bus route, and we began going visiting together every week. The workers consisted of our bus driver, Don Mills, a college student named Truitt Suhl, my dad, and me.

As we began to recruit riders and our route started to grow, I also began to learn something called compassion for others. I saw kids come on the bus wearing the same dirty, stained clothes every week because that was all they had. Yet, they wanted to come to church. Why? Because they knew that one man cared about them, and his name was "Brother Jack." They knew nothing of love and comfort, except on Sundays when they could ride "Bus 64" and be told over and over again how much we loved them. They craved this attention, and I often wondered why God didn't choose me to live in those lice-infested, seemingly God-forsaken slums and allow them to have my parents and live in a beautiful home.

The bus route is where I learned how to care for others and that everyone is important no matter what his last name is. It is where I learned what the true results of sin are and that nothing is as good as it looks on the billboards or on television. There is nothing attractive about walking into a one-room, back-alley apartment and stepping over a drunken mother and her boyfriend, kicking the beer cans out of the way, and trying to calm some frightened children and dress them for church. There is also nothing like the look in those children's eyes when they see us and know that they are going to a place for a few hours where they are loved and safe from fear.

You know, some people have real problems that are actually worse than having a well-known last name. My friend, Sarah Rodgers, has a dad who is in a wheelchair; and except for a miracle, he will never walk again. Every day she has to see him struggle through the everyday tasks that to most people would seem like nothing. Whenever I start to feel sorry for myself, I think of her, and somehow my problems just don't seem that big anymore.

Some of you cannot understand how someone could care or would want to care for people like this because you have never cared for anyone except yourself. You are the reason why "church staff kids" are labeled, and why it seems like no preacher's kids ever turn out right for God.

Yes, we are watched; yes, people expect a lot out of us, but remember, "...*unto whomsoever much is given, of him shall be much required.*" We have also been given a lot. Why don't we turn around and give to those who don't have as much as we do? Maybe our "burdens" will, all of a sudden, not seem like burdens at all!

CHAPTER THREE

Who Cares?

COMPASSION IS A WORD we have heard over and over, but do we really know what it means? What do you think compassion means?

I asked my husband what he thought it meant, and he said, "Compassion is caring for others more than yourself." Is there anyone about whom you care so much that you would do **anything** for him or her?

Jude 22 says, *"And of some have compassion, making a difference."* This verse must mean that if I am going to make a difference in anyone's life, I need to have compassion.

When I was in my teen years, some older girls were divided into two cliques. One clique was a group of girls who were the "good" girls. These girls were involved in everything at school and never got into trouble, but they also did not let anyone else join their little group.

The other clique of girls was not as involved, but they were very nice to others; and they even allowed others to hang around with them. Well, of course, the girls outside of the two cliques wanted to hang around the nice, but uninvolved girls. Why? Because this teenage group of girls had compassion. They cared for other people.

There is a song that I learned while in seventh grade that I want you to memorize and make into a theme for your teenage years:

"Let me be a little kinder;
Let me be a little blinder
To the faults of those around me;
Let me praise a little more.
Let me be when I am weary
Just a little bit more cheery,
Think a little more of my neighbor
And a little less of me."

Let me share three groups of people on whom we should have compassion:

1. Those who do you wrong. Has anyone ever done or said anything to you that you felt was wrong, and you never forgave her? In Psalm 78:38, the Bible tells how Jesus had compassion on us when we did Him wrong, and He forgave us. *"But he, being full of compassion, forgave their iniquity, and destroyed them not: yea, many a time turned he his anger away, and did not stir up all his wrath."* I think if He could forgive me for what I have done to Him, I can forgive that girl who hurt me.

2. Those who are hurting. Throughout my teenage years, I was surrounded by family and friends who loved me, and I always felt very loved. Some of you feel the same way, but many of you do not understand what being loved is like. You may, like many teens, have parents who have died, have gotten divorced, or who fight all of the time. Many of you are not surrounded by love. Someone needs to make sure those who do not live in a loving environment feel loved. They need to feel that someone cares and believes in them.

My Grandpa Hyles made this statement: "I believe every human being in the world would make it in life if he had one person who believed in him." Will you be that person who makes a difference in an individual's life because you believe in him?

3. Those whom you love. Your family and friends need to know you care about them. Unsaved family members could be saved if you showed them compassion. Your closest friends struggle just like you do, and they need compassion.

In closing, I want to share two stories. The first is about a grade school boy named Cliff. No one liked Cliff, and the kids at school made fun of him. One day, without telling anyone what he was going to do, he jumped out of a bus and killed himself. He died because he thought no one cared about him.

The next story is about Ruth, who was in my fifth grade class and who never said a word. Our teacher asked my friends and me to plan a birthday party for her. We had cake and ice cream, and everyone brought Ruth a gift. We spent the afternoon celebrating, and I had never seen her smile so much.

Ruth went through our schools and now attends

Hyles-Anderson College. Our fifth-grade teacher taught us a valuable lesson that day, and I'll never forget the compassion she had.

You don't have to be a teacher to change someone's life; in fact, why don't you change another's life with a note or a phone call? You never know—the person who needs your help might not be here tomorrow.

CHAPTER FOUR

Kindred Spirits

IF ANY OF YOU have ever watched the "Anne of Green Gables" videos or read the books by Lucy Maud Montgomery, then you have heard Anne talk about "kindred spirits." Just like Anne and Diana were kindred spirits in these stories, there were some kindred spirits in the Bible, too.

In Samuel the Bible says that the soul of Jonathan was knit with the soul of David. *"And it came to pass, when he had made an end of speaking unto Saul, that the soul of Jonathan was knit with the soul of David, and Jonathan loved him as his own soul."* (I Samuel 18:1) Jonathan and David were "kindred spirits." In the book of Ruth, the Bible talks about Ruth cleaving to her mother-in-law Naomi. *"And they lifted up their voice, and wept again: and Orpah kissed her mother in law; but Ruth clave unto her.*" (Ruth 1:14) Ruth and Naomi were "kindred spirits."

Have you ever met anyone who you felt was a kindred spirit? Maybe you had just moved to a new area, or maybe your family was going through a hard time. Someone crossed your path and became your closest friend! I believe that God sends certain people into our lives sometimes to help us, whether we are lonely or have been hurt by another or maybe are just having a tough day.

I have met some people whom I believe God sent into my life to help me get through something, and I felt very loved by those people. These are people I can call whenever I want to laugh or who will cry with me when I need to cry. They are the ones who I know would be there in a second if I needed them or if something tragic happened to me.

Who are your "kindred spirits"? Who is that one you can always count on to be there and in whom you can always confide?

Not only does God give us special friends, but He uses us to help those who are hurting, too. I read a true story about a teenage girl who went to a large public school and felt like no one cared about her. Day after day she went from class to class feeling lonely and like no one really cared about her.

One particular day was especially hard, so she decided she would just end it all. She did not think life was worth living. She went through the day at school, got home, and as soon as she walked in the door, the phone rang. She picked it up, and a girl from school was on the line. "Hi," she said, "I just felt like I should call you to see how you are doing. I wanted to let you know that I care about you."

The girl who had been contemplating suicide began crying and thanked her friend for calling. "You saved my life," she sobbed. "I was just about to kill myself."

Whose life are you helping to save today? Who is the lonely girl in your school who thinks she has no friends and thinks life is not worth living? Are you the "kindred spirit" upon whom she can depend, or are you killing her spirit?

If you are lonely today, remember that Jesus is your very best friend. He is the only One Who can and will always be there for you when no one else can be. Jesus is **the** kindred Spirit, and He wants so much to be close to you.

- Do you talk to Him?
- Do you read His Word?
- Have you told anyone about Him lately?

Mrs. Marlene Evans, the founder of Christian Womanhood, used to say, "Breathe life into people!" Are you giving life to people, or are you taking it away? Let's be a "kindred spirit" to someone, and if God sends someone into your path to help you, thank Him for the gift of friendship.

CHAPTER FIVE

True Friends Forever

IF YOU COULD PICK anyone in the world to be your best friend, whom would you choose? If you could meet with anyone you wanted and chat for 15 minutes, who would it be? There are several people I would love to meet such as Mrs. Ronald Reagan, our former President's wife, and ask her how she had a successful marriage while being married to the President of the United States. I would also have liked to have met Mrs. John R. Rice, who was married to Dr. John R. Rice, one of the greatest leaders of fundamentalism who ever lived. I think it would have been fun to have met Princess Diana also. Even though she was not the best of examples, many women were interested in watching her. She had an elegance about her, and many in England seemed to admire her.

These ladies were considered successful in the eyes of Christianity or in the eyes of the world for their dedication and accomplishments; yet, I think if we really had gotten to know each of them, we would have realized they were just as human and normal as we are. They are or were also just as human and normal as your friends are. The only reason we do not see our friends through the same eyes as we see those whom we have never personally met but would do anything to meet is that we **know** our friends.

True friends are those who decide to love you no matter what you do or how you disappoint them. True friends are the ones who are there for you when the worst thing that could possibly happen happens. True friends are the ones who weep with you when you weep and laugh with you when you want to laugh, and they are the ones with whom you can be completely yourself.

When my friend, Sheri Dalton, and I get together, all we do is laugh and have fun! Sometimes we laugh so hard we have to lie flat on the floor! That is the best way to laugh—when you are lying flat on the floor where you can laugh the hardest. (Everyone should try it sometime.) Sheri is a lot of fun to be around; yet, she has also been there for me through times when all I could do was cry. She has also been there in times when it was probably hard for her to be my friend. No friend is going to be perfect, and if you go looking for one who is, you will be looking for a long time. People are human, and they do make mistakes. Why don't we treat our friends as well as those whom we most admire? After all, they have chosen to be our friend, so why don't we treat that friend with respect? Are you saying that your friend made a bad choice when she chose you as a friend?

I have some of the greatest friends in the whole world, yet we have had our struggles, too. The greatest thing about my friends is that they chose to be my friend—in spite of our struggles. Rachel (Alberts) Richards, Linda (Young) Tutton, and Sheri (Nocito) Dalton were my best friends through high school. Heidi (Pickering) Carillo, Mindy Wertz, and Annie Kimmel have also been true friends to me. These are the friends who were there for me when my Grandpa Hyles died and who stood beside me and cried with me when they didn't know what to say or do. God has given me some of the greatest friends on the face of the earth, and in return, I am supposed to be a friend to them as well as to others who need someone to care about them.

Some of you do not know the joy of having a true friend because you have never been a friend to anyone. The Bible does say that in order to *have* friends, you must first *be* a friend. Stop looking for friends and start being a friend. You will be surprised how many friends will find you.

Now I want you to ask yourself a few questions.

- "What kind of friend am I?"
- "Am I the right kind of influence on my friend?"
- "Am I the kind of person with whom parents tell their children not to hang around?"
- "Am I choosing the right kind of friends?"

Proverbs 18:24 says, *"A man that hath friends must shew himself friendly: and there is a friend that sticketh closer than a brother."* If you make God your best Friend, then He will give you the right kind of friends.

The first part of that verse says if you want to have friends, you have to be a friendly person. How do you treat those who are your friends? Do you treat them with respect, or do you treat them like dirt every time they make a mistake and don't treat you like you think you deserve to be treated? Remember, they did choose to be your friend. Was it a good choice or a bad choice? Only you can determine that.

Decide today to make God your best Friend, and be a true friend to your friends. Your friends are going to let you down sometimes, but God will always be your Friend.

CHAPTER SIX

Tennis or Ice Cream?

WHICH DO YOU LIKE better—ice cream or tennis? Would you rather play volleyball or go to Hawaii? Do you like Mexican food or sandals better? You are probably thinking I have gone completely crazy right now and that I am not making any sense at all, and you are exactly right! (Well, I am not completely crazy!)

How can you compare these things with each other when they are so different? It just doesn't make sense, and neither does it make any sense when you start comparing yourself to someone else!

Psalm 139:14 says, *"I will praise thee; for I am fearfully and wonderfully made…."* God created—from nothing—each one of us uniquely and beautifully in His eyes. When we criticize ourselves or always focus on our "flaws," we are really telling God that we are not happy with how He made us.

I had a friend in high school who seemed so perfect, and she seemed to do everything right all the time. She was a great seamstress, and I hate to sew! She was very smart, and I had to study for hours to pass a test. She was the tall, blonde, and beautiful girl that I was not. In my eyes, I was just of average height with average brown hair, average brown eyes, average weight, and I just felt pretty "average."

I finally had to face the fact that I was never going to be tall and blonde, and I wasn't exactly heading toward sewing my own clothes!

The Bible says in II Corinthians 10:12 that "...they *measuring themselves by themselves, and comparing themselves among themselves, are not wise.*" That verse means that when we look at another who seems to be better at everything than we are or who just seems to have it all together, we are not being wise. Maybe she is the one who is the most popular girl in school, or perhaps she is the one who gets all the dates, and maybe you feel like "plain Jane" who is never noticed because "there is nothing special about you."

I had to come to the point where I realized that if God had wanted me to be "tall, blonde, and beautiful," He would have created me like that. If He had wanted me to be a seamstress, He would have given me a love for sewing (which He did not!), and if He had wanted me to be brilliant, He would have made me that way. Instead, I had to start focusing on the talents I did have and develop those to the best of my ability.

One of the greatest days of my life was the day I realized that I don't have to be like anyone else, and I don't have to be good at what other people are good at—I just have to be myself.

The moment I realized that God created me for a special and unique reason and I didn't have to try to be something I was not, I felt a great peace and calm. You see, God has something so special for you to do, and He created only you to do it. He has someone so special for you to marry, and He created only you for him. God has some children so special for you to rear someday, and He created only you to rear them.

Trust me! You really are special to God, and I promise you, He loves you just the way you are. If God can love you and me with all of our mistakes and weaknesses, then maybe we can love ourselves and each other, too.

CHAPTER SEVEN

I'll Trust When I Cannot See

"I care not today what tomorrow may bring.
If shadow, or sunshine, or rain.
The Lord I know ruleth o'er everything.
And all of my worry is vain.

Living by faith in Jesus above;
Trusting, confiding in His great love.
From all harm safe in His sheltering arms,
I'm living by faith, and I feel no alarm."

I HAVE HEARD THIS SONG sung over and over, and I even like to sing it when I am driving or when I am somewhere by myself. (I prefer to sing just to myself, and I am sure everyone else is glad I sing just to myself, too!) I sing this song often, but today I actually took the time to think about what I was singing, and my thoughts made me realize how much we need these words.

My mom gave a talk to some ladies about how faith is seeing what other people cannot see. Having faith in someone is believing that person can become something that she herself does not even think she can become. Faith is believing that Jesus died for us on the cross and asking Him to come into our heart. Faith is all that it takes to be saved. My Grandpa Hyles once said that he believed every human being in the world would make it in life if he had one person who believed in him.

Faith is also trusting in God when it seems He is so far away. It is trusting Him and depending on Him when you find out that you have leukemia or when you learn your mother is dying of cancer and has only a few months to live. It is believing God has someone special for you who will make you so much happier than the "wonderful" guy you were dating who is crushing you as you watch him date your "best friend." Faith is trusting that God knows what He is doing when everything in your life falls apart.

Faith, like confidence, determination, and character, can be built, and it can also be torn apart. God uses people to help strengthen our faith in Him. Likewise, Satan uses people to tear down our faith in God and to cause us to trust in ourselves. When you go through something hard in your life and you don't know what to do, do you run to those people who judge you or criticize you or don't care about you? No! You run to people you know you can trust and whom you can count on to be there for you. You go to those in whom you have faith.

Let me ask you: are you helping build faith, or are you doing a great job of tearing down people? A family I know is going through some problems and having a tough time. Recently, I heard someone say about this family, "They are so weird!" Little does that judgmental person know what that family is facing in their lives; they are struggling and do not know what to do.

My Grandpa Hyles had a motto by which he lived: "Be good to everybody because everybody is having a tough time." Are you living by this motto? Are you so busy labeling people and judging them that you don't have time to help or love anyone? Are you so into yourself that you don't even notice that the girl at school whom everyone picks on goes home and cries herself to sleep every night of her life?

I know a girl who has an unsaved dad and a mother who is dying of cancer. Obviously that girl is having a very hard time. Her faith is wavering right now, and she does not know what to do. If someone were to take the time to talk to her and comfort her, her faith and trust might become stronger; but if someone tells her she is strange and does not quite fit in, that could destroy her faith in God for the rest of her life.

Are you a faith builder or a faith destroyer? Are your words and actions tearing down or building up? You could save or destroy a life by what you say or do today. Let's choose to save a life because Someone did choose to save us.

CHAPTER EIGHT

I Was Scared Out of My Mind!

WHEN YOU WERE SMALL, do you remember being afraid of the dark? Did you have to have a night light in your room so you could see? What was it that made you afraid? It was not being able to see what was there.

My dad and my brother (and now my husband) go deer hunting every year with my Grandpa Schaap in Michigan for a few days. During one of those trips when I was 15, I awoke around 1:00 a.m. to the sound of bags rattling downstairs. I knew my dad had left some ammunition for his rifles in some bags in the basement, and when I awoke, I heard "someone" going through the bags. I was so scared that I immediately reached in the drawer for my dad's handgun, woke up my mom, and told her I was going downstairs to see who was in the house. Obviously, my mom was very startled to awaken to the sight of her daughter holding a gun and telling her someone was in the house, so she followed me to the top of the stairs.

Once I reached the stairs, I was too scared to go down, so I turned on the light, thinking that whoever it was would stop moving, but the noise continued. Now I was really scared—the kind of scared where you go to scream and nothing comes out. I was frightened out of my mind.

After I contacted the Lake County Police Department, two squad cars finally made it to the house, after getting lost, and thoroughly searched the premises. After about 10 minutes of careful investigation, they came out and told us that everything was okay. The "intruder" happened to be a mouse that had somehow found its way into our basement! We felt like idiots, and I am sure the police at the station had a good laugh that night as they told about two "crazy women" who were scared of a mouse!

What made me so afraid that I could not even go

downstairs and see what the noise was? I was afraid of what I could not see, and fear drove me to act like a crazy person who could not think straight.

That is exactly how Satan wants you to react to the problems you face in your life. He wants to scare you into "going crazy" because only then will he have control of your mind. Fear is the opposite of trust, which we are supposed to have in God; and when we are afraid, we are showing our lack of confidence in God.

Do you think God is big enough to take care of you today? What are you afraid of that is causing you to do or say things that do not make sense? Does Satan have a grip on your mind today?

I do not believe that people who are saved and have Jesus living inside them can be demon-possessed, but I do believe they can be influenced by the Devil, and one of the most powerful tools he uses is the mind. Fatigue, worry, stress, and fear all wear down the mind until we can hardly think straight, and that is when he likes to attack us.

What do you fear? I do not mean phobias like being afraid of the dark or fear of heights; I am talking about fears like your mother is going to die from her cancer; fear that the guy you like might break up with you and date someone else or that he is not the one God wants you to marry; fear of taking a stand for right because your friends might make fun of you and not want to hang around you any more; fear that if you start reading your Bible and actually start talking to God that you will be convicted of your rock music and feel like you need to stop listening to it.

A teenage guy who is very troubled has been coming to church with my brother as a result of a new teen ministry that our church has started. The other day my brother went to pick him up, and the song, "It Is Well With My Soul" was playing in his CD player. The young man quickly asked my brother to turn off "that music" because it bothered him. Why did that music bother him? He was afraid that God might speak to his heart if he listened to it, and after all, he does not believe in God. He is afraid to change because he is so deep into his sin that he cannot think straight. He did not like the words because everything is not "well with his soul."

Of what are you afraid that is keeping you from

trusting in God? I talked to a girl the other day who told me that she is afraid to go to the college that God wants her to go to because her boyfriend is going to another college and she might lose him. My friend, where is your trust in God? Do you not believe He is a big enough God to handle that problem? Do you not believe He will lead you right into His will if you trust Him? But first you must trust Him.

Trust Him with that thing that you are so afraid of today. Give your problem to Him and leave it in His hands. Stop worrying and fretting and find a peace that only comes from trusting in God.

CHAPTER NINE

Overcoming Obstacles

HAVE YOU EVER BEEN walking while not looking where you were going and tripped and fell flat on your face? Isn't it so embarrassing? A couple of weeks ago I was tutoring a boy named Nicholas, in my junior high class, who is in a wheelchair, and I was trying to walk around him when, without seeing his foot in front of me, I tripped and went flying through the air, landing face first on the floor! The gum that WAS in my mouth went flying, landing somewhere ahead of me, and of course, my class thought that was hilarious!

Now this story is funny (because it did not happen to you), but the truth is that if I had been looking where I was headed and not talking to someone while turned around, I never would have fallen in the first place. Even though it was quite embarrassing, tripping over something we can see and falling on the ground is better than tripping over something that Satan puts in our path and falling into sin or even ruining our lives.

If you will look up Hebrews 12:1, you will find a verse that talks about running a race and setting aside the weights that pull us down. In I Corinthians there is a verse that talks about how everyone runs a race, but only one person gets the prize. Why, if so many run the race, does only one person get the prize? Many teens do not finish their "race" because they trip over the weights or obstacles that Satan puts in their path. What kind of "weights" could Satan put in your path to keep you from running your race? How about the weight of parents getting a divorce? This weight has kept some teens from even thinking about serving God, and it has caused some to even end their lives. Another common weight is the weight of clinging to the wrong guy because he accepts you like you are, and you feel you really need that security.

Let's take a look at some weights that are not so obvious, like the weight of self-analyzing. Self-analysis means constantly looking at yourself and saying, "I'm so fat," or "I am so dumb," or "I wish I could be like her."

This weight will pull you out of your race very fast, and comparing yourself with others only makes you feel worse about yourself. You will tear yourself down until you are an emotional basket case and you have convinced yourself that you are completely and positively worthless. Girls, this is a lie of Satan because you are precious and priceless to God. *"How precious also are thy thoughts unto me, O God! how great is the sum of them!"* (Psalm 139:17) Do not let the Devil fool you into thinking that you are not worth anything.

Satan uses many other weights to try to pull us out of our race, like self-pity, the death of people we love, financial problems, circumstances that are beyond our control, and the list goes on and on. Then how, if there are so many weights to "trip" us, can we possibly make it to the end?

The answer is found in the song "Turn Your Eyes Upon Jesus" and in trusting when you cannot see the way. The answer is trust. Remember when you were a little girl and someone told you about Jesus and showed you how you could go to Heaven someday? You did not doubt the person for a second, and you eagerly bowed your head and trusted Christ. Now that you are a teenager and you are seeing a little of the reality of life, your faith is being shaken. You need to look deep in your soul and find that childlike faith you once had, dig it out, blow off the dust, and learn to trust in God again. You need to open up your hymnal and relearn the words to "Tis so sweet to trust in Jesus, just to take Him at His Word...."

Maybe you need to get your Bible and look up every verse with the words "faith" or "trust" and read them over and over again. Pray that God will give you the faith you need to overcome the obstacle you are facing.

Whatever you are facing, remember God is stronger than Satan, and He will always be right by your side to hold your hand and lead you through to the end. And once you reach the end, He will be there to give you your prize and say, "Well done, good and faithful servant."

CHAPTER TEN

Is God Real?

HOW MUCH HAVE YOU talked to your boyfriend this week? How many letters have you written to him this month? How many hours have you talked to your friends on the phone? How many hours have you spent shopping or going out with your friends this week?

After you answer those questions, I want you to answer this series of questions:

- How many hours have you spent with God this week?
- How many hours have you spent talking to Him?
- How many times have you read His letter to you this month?
- How many times have you told Him you love Him today?

If you are like most teenagers, the first few questions were probably a lot easier to answer than the last few were. Why? Because we really do not believe that God is real. Oh, He is somewhere up in Heaven helping the really spiritual people, but He seems as far away to us as a foreign country. We don't talk to Him because we do not really believe He hears us and will always answer our prayers.

What if I told you God is going to put your parents' marriage back together, or what if I told you He is going to heal your grandfather's cancer? Would you talk to God if you knew He would bring your brother back to church or show you exactly whom you are going to marry?

You see, we believe God hears other people's prayers, but we don't believe He hears our prayers. We've heard about all of the miracles God performed in the Bible days, but somehow we don't think He still does that today.

I talked to the girls in my Sunday school class about making God real in their lives, and I told them to start praying for something that, if God answered it, would prove to them that God was real. Then we decided to pray every night for God to answer our prayers, no matter where we were or what we were doing at 9:00 p.m. We also began fasting one meal a week for God to answer our prayer. Did God really hear us? Well, let me tell you some things God did answer:

- A mother who was dying of cancer discovered her cancer was in remission.
- A grandma who was unsaved and dying accepted Christ on her deathbed.
- A cousin who could not get pregnant for six years learned that she is having a baby.
- An aunt who was dying of a rare disease went to the doctor, and he told her that God had healed her.
- A mom and dad who were separated got back together and are happy.
- A truck that wouldn't start and was needed for a ride to school started and ran all year.
- A family needed a house in a better neighborhood, and they found what they needed.

Do you think these girls who are juniors in high school think God is real? Would you think God was real if He healed your mom's cancer? These girls know that God is real because He answered their prayers.

What prayer do you want to see God answer in your life? What would it take for you to believe there is a God in Heaven Who loves you more than anyone in the world and Who hears you when you pray?

If you really want to see God work or if there is something so heavy on your heart and you really don't see any way out, please decide to prove God and see for yourself how real God is to **you**.

I gave this talk at our teen camp, and I asked the girls to write down a request. We are also praying together for each other every night at 9:00 p.m. Some of the things on the list are going to take a miracle for God to answer. How many do I believe He will answer? Every one! It may take time, but I believe in a real God Who loves us and Who loves a challenge.

I beg you to ask God for something big from Him and prove that He's not just your pastor's God or your parents' God, but He's your God.

CHAPTER ELEVEN

What You See Is What You Get

WHEN YOU SEE A girl walking down the street or in the mall with dyed black hair, black nails and lipstick, a ghostly white face, completely dressed in black, wearing a dog collar set with spikes around her neck, wearing five to ten black bracelets on each wrist and several chains around the pockets of her baggy black pants, do you think to yourself, "What a lady! Why, she must be a Christian!" To be sure, that girl may love God with all of her heart and be surrendered to the mission field, but you would never know that fact by just looking at her.

When you see a nun dressed in her plain black dress and a white veil on her head with no makeup or very little if any jewelry, carrying her big family Bible and looking to Heaven with her hands folded in prayer, do you think to yourself, "She must be a wild woman; she looks like a prostitute!" She may be a very naughty woman inside, but you would never know it by just looking at her.

When you walk down the street or around the mall in your outfit, talking to your friends, what do people think when they see you? Do they see your knee-length skirt and modest shirt or sweater and think, "She must be a Christian!"; or do they see your jeans and t-shirt from Abercrombie and Fitch or Hollister and think you are just another sloppy, typical teenager? When guys look at you, do they think, "What a pure, innocent girl!"; or do they take one look at you and think, "I could get anything I want out of that girl—she's definitely for sale."

You may not think what you wear is that important. After all, people should not judge you just by what they see. Maybe they shouldn't, but that is the way people are. The Bible says, *"…man looketh on the outward appearance, but the LORD looketh on the heart."* (I Samuel 16:7) There is a popular Christian song that talks about what the world sees in a Christian, and that would include our appearance. The following are the words to the chorus:

"When the world looks at me, do they see Jesus?
When the world looks at me, what do they see?
Do they see hope? Do they see love?
     Do they see charity?
When the world looks at me, what do they see?"

Whether or not you like it, people judge you by what they see with their eyes. Nobody except for God knows what is in your heart, but what is in your heart usually does come out. You may be the most pure-minded girl, but if you wear tops that are too low and reveal too much, men are not going to see your pure mind; they are going to see your body and think you want to be immoral.

Men have a hard enough time keeping their minds pure with all of the filthy commercials, billboards, and ungodly women in the world, and they do not need Christian girls and ladies to add to the problem. The Bible says that if a man looks at a woman and thinks bad thoughts about her in his mind, then he has committed a very sinful act in his heart. Are you wearing something that causes someone else's husband to think wicked thoughts about you? Even the most perverted man who has been immoral time after time, when it comes time for him to choose someone to marry for the rest of his life, wants someone who is pure and clean—someone who has saved herself just for him.

Did you know that men think very differently than women? Clothing we think is perfectly fine and so "stylish and cute" may actually not be appropriate to wear around the opposite gender. Sometimes I will not wear the things I think are so adorable and trendy because my husband does not feel comfortable with my wearing them. I know you do not yet have a husband, and your boyfriend might want you to wear things that "catch his eye," so a great way to make sure you are wearing the right thing is to ask your dad how you look. Ask him if something is too tight or too low and if it is appropriate to wear out. I'm sure if your dad is anything like mine, he will make sure you look right because you are his precious girl, and the last thing he wants is for some jerk to put his hands on you or have lustful thoughts about you!

A good rule to go by is, "If it's doubtful, don't do it," or "If it's questionable, don't wear it!" Remember, you want that Prince Charming to be saving himself for you, but are you saving yourself for him?

CHAPTER TWELVE

Every Relationship Begins With God

"I GOT UP EARLY ONE morning and rushed right into the day,

I had so much to acccomplish, I didn't have time to pray.

Problems just tumbled about me, and heavier became each task.

'Why doesn't God help me?' I wondered.

He answered, 'You didn't ask.'

I woke up early this morning and paused before entering the day,

I had so much to accomplish, I had to take time to pray."

This portion of a poem is one of my favorites because it shows how important it is to have a relationship with God.

- What is the difference between a happy teenager and one who is depressed and suicidal? A relationship with God!

- How do you get along with your family and friends? Through a relationship with God.

- What can help you to pass your classes, receive no demerits, and give you respect for authority? A relationship with God.

- How can you get the wisdom you need to date and marry right and to find God's will? You probably already know the answer—through a relationship with God.

You see, every successful relationship begins with a close walk with God. My dad and my grandpa, Dr. Jack Hyles, have both used the illustrations on the next page.

End of Life Without God

Figure 1 illustrates the relationship between a mother and a daughter without their having a relationship with God. Their relationship never grows any closer because they have never developed a relationship with God.

End of Life With God

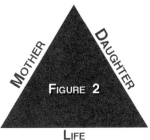

Figure 2 illustrates how a mother and a daughter can become close if they draw close to God.

Just in case you don't understand the drawings, let me explain:

A girl talked to me the other day about her relationship with her mom. She is a good girl, but she is having a difficult time getting along with her mother, and she does not know what to do.

Although I think she needs to get along with her mom, I believe the real problem lies within her heart and in her relationship with her Saviour. The Bible said about Jesus when He lived on this earth that He *"…increased in wisdom and stature, and in favour with God and man."* (Luke 2:52) Because Jesus was in favor with God, He was also in favor with man.

At this writing, we are preparing for our annual Valentine banquet, and some of the young men have already begun asking girls to go with them. Let's say a couple has been dating for a while (by the way, we do not promote serious high school dating) and the guy assumes his girlfriend is going with him, so he does not even bother to ask her. He pays for two tickets, rents a tuxedo, and buys a bouquet of flowers and a box of candy.

When the night of the banquet comes, he shows up at her house to pick her up. To his surprise, no one answers the door, so he knocks again. He finally decides to call her on her cell phone, and he finds out she went shopping with some friends because she did not think he wanted to take her!

I liked Todd Weber the first time I met him.

However, our relationship never would have begun had he not asked me on our very first date—a Chicago boat ride! I wanted to date him, but he first had to ask. A guy may want to go to the Valentine banquet with his girlfriend, but he still has to ask her.

God desperately wants to have a relationship with you, but **you** have to ask Him. He does not force anyone to be close to Him; He wants us to choose to be with Him. God also wants to help you with your other relationships in life.

- He wants you to love, respect, and like your parents.

- He wants you to respect and obey your teachers.

- He wants you to love and pray for your friends.

- He wants you to have a close relationship with your husband some day.

All you have to do is ask Him!

So, if I may give some advice to the girl who is having a hard time getting along with her mom (and anyone who is struggling with a relationship), work on your relationship with God, and every other relationship you have will take care of itself. God wants to be close to all of us; all we have to do is ask.

CHAPTER THIRTEEN

If I Could Look Inside Your Heart

IF I COULD LOOK inside your heart,
What would I really see?
A heart that's full of bitterness,
Hatred and jealousy;
A heart that's painted black with sin,
Rebellion and deceit,
From years of living in a world
Of loss and great defeat?

If I could look inside your heart,
What would I really see?
A heart that aches with constant pain
From breaking endlessly;

Did sorrow come into your life
So very long ago
And rip, and tear, and pull apart
The heart you used to know?

Has tragedy come in your life,
Or sickness, pain, and loss;
You try to hide the hurt inside
Of carrying your cross?
Do you go home each night to find
The burden that you had
You try to find true happiness
Yet always feel so sad.

You always wonder when your night will end
And turn to glorious day.
Yet tears will just not cease to fall
Pain will not go away.
If I could look inside your heart,
What would I dare to find?
A heart that's high and lifted up
With arrogance and pride?

A mind so filled with thoughts of self
No room is left for those
Who are the hurting, broken ones
Who carry pain and woes.
A life that touches no one else
Except for number one,
With no compassion, care, and love
For even God's own Son?

Or, if I looked inside your heart,
Would I see joy and love—
The kind of everlasting joy
That comes from God above?
Would I see strength for each new day
And grace for every hour?
And would I find a sample of God's everlasting
    power?

Should I peer in and take a look
Could I expect to see
A glimpse of Jesus Christ, the One
Who bled and died for me?
Would I look in and see the One

To Whom we all belong.
And hear the sounds of Heaven ring
In praise and worship song?

I hope if I could look inside
Each heart of yours today
That I would find the heart of one
Who has chosen God's way.
I hope I could not find one full
Of bitterness and strife
Or find it full of emptiness
Without God in your life.

What would a greater One than I
Find in your heart today?
For He can see inside each one;
I wonder what He'd say?
Would He be disappointed in
The kind of life you live?
Have you rejected Him and all
The love He's tried to give?

I hope if He were looking in,
He would say, "Well done,
I see the face of One I love,
My own begotten Son."

– Jaclynn Weber

I wrote this poem for you and for me. I hope your heart and mine are right with God today. My dad once said that we should not wait until a youth revival, a conference, or camp to get right with God, but instead, we should make sure our heart is right with Him every day.

Do you know Him today? If you don't, I beg you to get saved today. If you know Him but have wandered far away from Him, it's never too late to come back home. He is waiting with open arms, and He wants to be close to you. Make this song your own and come home to Him today.

"I've wandered far away from God,
Now I'm coming home;
The paths of sin too long I've trod,
Lord, I'm coming home.

Coming home, coming home,
Nevermore to roam.
Open wide Thine arms of love
Lord, I'm coming home."